ROCKETS, SAND, AND AMALGAM

ROBERT L. ENGELMEIER

ROCKETS, SAND, AND AMALGAM

MEMOIRS FROM THE REAR

Charleston, SC
www.PalmettoPublishing.com

Rockets, Sand, and Amalgam

First Edition

Hardcover ISBN: 979-8-8229-1910-5
Paperback ISBN: 979-8-8229-1911-2
eBook ISBN: 979-8-8229-1912-9

MEMOIRS OF A YOUNG DENTIST'S SERVICE DURING THE VIETNAM WAR

ROBERT L ENGELMEIER BS, DMD, MS, FACP, FAAMP
COLONEL USAF/RET

*"Be who you are and say what you feel,
because those that mind don't matter and
those who matter don't mind."*

—DR. SEUSS

DEDICATION

To Vietnam veterans:

"Welcome home, brothers..."

TABLE OF CONTENTS

INTRODUCTION

A merica's involvement in Vietnam began shortly after World War II, when President Truman elected to deploy thirty-five military advisors there in support of France and its efforts to reestablish French Indochina. Those advisors were not sent there in a combat role but rather to supervise the support of US military equipment valued then at $10 million. The war in Vietnam lasted over two decades for American forces. However, that was just the last segment of a nearly century-long-conflict involving France and its efforts to consolidate Vietnam, Laos, and Cambodia into a French colony. Following World War II and the expulsion of the Japanese, the people of Southeast Asia wanted independence for their respective countries, while the French expected a return to colonialism. To avert a domino effect of communism overwhelming those countries, Presidents Truman and Eisenhower supported the French with military aid and advisors but not ground troops. After fighting a decade long war of insurgency, the French were finally defeated in 1954 at Dien Bien Phu, in Northwestern

Vietnam on the Laotian border. At that point, they relinquished all claims in Southeast Asia. The US then entered the war that France had abandoned. The motive was to prevent Ho Chi Minh from overpowering democratic South Vietnam and uniting all of Vietnam under communism. By 1960, the number of US military advisors in Vietnam had increased from 327 to 685. President Kennedy sent an additional 400 US Army Green Beret advisors to Vietnam in 1961. By late 1963, the number of US military advisors in country had ballooned to 16,000. Shortly after becoming president, Lyndon Johnson decided to "Americanize" the war in Vietnam. By 1965, he had ordered 50,000 combat troops to be deployed there. The rest is a controversial and bloody history.

During the American Vietnam War era (mid 1965–mid 1975), 9,087,000 individuals served on active duty with the US Military. Approximately 2,594,000 served within the borders of Vietnam. Between 1–1.6,000,000 of them served in combat roles. Draftees comprised 25 percent of those exposed to direct combat and 30.4 percent of those draftees were killed in action. The total number of Americans lost in the war was 58,318. Of those, 47,359 died in direct combat. Additional statistics report that: 303,704 were wounded, 766 became POWs (114 of whom died in captivity), and 2,338 were listed as missing.

It has been generally theorized that it ideally takes ten individuals (in the rear) to support 7 fighting men on the front lines (a "tooth-to-tail" ratio of 1 to 1.42). Though statistics vary, it seems that the ratio during the Vietnam War varied between 1.6-2.6 support people for each fighting man in Vietnam. History has shown that the better the tail support, the more effective front-line fighters have been. Though in the rear, hospital and other support personnel in Vietnam often found themselves in peril due to long range enemy rockets and suicide "sapper" attacks.

Armed forces' physical standards have long been established to keep military members fit for world-wide deployment. That has consistently included a disease-free mouth. Dental pain and infection can greatly reduce a soldier's effectiveness. The responsibility of nondeployed dental service members has been the restoration and maintenance of service members' oral health prior to any deployment. The expectation of deployed dental corps clinicians has been to keep servicemen free of dental disease and pain while serving in remote assignments. At the 483rd USAF Dental Clinic, we saw score upon score of young draftees, particularly those from poor inner-city neighborhoods and rural communities, whose deployment had been expedited despite multiple large dental caries, partially impacted third molars, abscessed teeth, and acute gingival problems. None of their problems had been addressed during basic or advanced infantry training. Their restoration had been left for the dentists stationed "in country." The excessive time that those troops had to spend in a Vietnam dental chair robbed them and their units of time that should have been spent fulfilling their assigned missions. Grunts assigned to relentless patrols in the bush or at remote fire bases often had to endure considerable dental torment until they could get to a base camp with a dental facility. Only about half of the patients at our Cam Ranh Bay Air Force clinic were Air Force members. Nearly 40 percent were Army (mostly draftees). The remaining were a mixture of Navy, Marine Corps, and contracted civilians. We understood the burden that many GIs had to endure fighting the war while suffering significant dental pain. We worked many long hours doing our best to try to keep up. This anthology of some Vietnam War memories is not intended to be a report of long days of endless fillings and extractions. It is a collection of situations probably never experienced by my peers who never saw Southeast Asia service.

I was a young Air Force captain and a recent graduate of the University of Pittsburgh School of Dental Medicine. I had been assigned to the 483rd USAF Hospital at Cam Ranh Bay, Vietnam just three months after graduation. I had received no basic training per se, only a short orientation course at Sheppard AFB in West Texas that consisted of many instructional movies and a bit of marching. That was followed by one-week of small arms training at Hamilton AFB on the northwestern shore of San Francisco Bay. I had arrived in Vietnam with competent understanding of my responsibilities as a general dentist, but with very little understanding of the military. As these stories attest, that ignorance did lay the ground work for my getting into a bit of trouble from time to time.

BEKINS

I arrived at the fourteenth Aerial Port at Cam Ranh Bay Air Force Base in late August of 1970. As I deplaned, I was met by the clinic oral surgeon, Lt. Col. Jim Wooten. Since it was near the end of the working day that Saturday afternoon, there was no one available to sign me in. He drove me to one of the empty hospital wards and instructed me to sleep as long as possible to overcome the jet lag and to sign-in at the hospital orderly room on Monday morning. The ward contained two long rows of freshly changed beds. It was windowless, very dark, and fortunately air conditioned. I slept soundly for fourteen hours. The 483rd USAF Hospital was the second largest Air Force hospital. It contained 475 beds with an additional one hundred bed casualty staging area. There was a large, two-story main building, surrounded by multiple Quonset hut units housing the wards and several conjoined metal modular buildings. All structures were interconnected by exterior covered sidewalks. Since Cam Ranh peninsula was a giant sand dune, transporting patients, as well as walking between the hospital buildings, would have been extremely difficult without the concrete walkways.

After awakening on Sunday morning, I wandered around the hospital structures for a while before I found an NCO on duty who called the dental officer on call (DOD). He met me, walked me back to the hospital officer hooch area, and introduced me to some of the other assigned dentists. They invited me to go with them to a party that evening at the Bekins Air Van Facility.

Bekins had a very large warehouse complex that bordered the flightline. Besides all the cargo that they moved between the West Coast, Philippines, and Vietnam, they also moved all personal hold baggage of incoming and departing troops. Somewhere in their warehouse complex, there was a large party room that hosted frequent drunken bashes of military, contracted civilian workers, nurses and doughnut dollies, visiting politicians, and entertainers at the various military clubs on the peninsula... in short, anyone who befriended John Cherrington, the manager. Of course, I went. I was still wearing my 1505s (tan US Air Force summer uniform) because I had not yet in-processed and received issued jungle fatigue uniforms. I did have one pair of Levi's and one sports shirt in my suitcase, so I decided to wear them. Quite a few attended the party. I was greeted by John, our gracious host who spent a considerable amount of time talking to me. He too was twenty-six years old and hailed from Southern California. There was plenty of beer on tap along with a well-stocked bar. In the center of an incredible buffet table was a huge silver caldron of what I assumed were simmering "beef" cubes. Since I had not eaten for nearly two days, that table with the simmering meat was the focus of my attention. I was never quite clear who the young ladies there were but each one was surrounded by half a dozen horny guys. I only talked to people who shared the buffet table with me. Though that meat appeared to be beef, it was certainly more tender and uniquely seasoned than anything that I had ever experienced. When I asked my host about it, he smiled and said that he would tell me later. Thinking that it was probably something exotic like monkey, I kept munching those incredibly delicious morsels.

BEKINS AIR VAN MANAGER'S HOUSE IN THE CENTER
OF THE WAREHOUSE QUADRANGLE.

As I washed it all down with plenty of draft beer, I lost all sense of time. I panicked when I realized that my ride had left without me. Nearly everyone was gone. I was alone and had no idea where I was. Since I had not yet signed in, no one officially knew that I was in Vietnam. But my host came to the rescue. He took me outside and pointed to what looked like a typical ranch-style house back home sitting in the center of a massive parking lot. That huge lot for trucks was surrounded by a quadrangle of the company's spacious warehouses. John instructed me to go to the side door of the house, knock hard, and his roommate would let me in to spend the night there. John assured me that he would personally drive me to the hospital orderly room to officially sign in in the morning.

As I staggered across that very dark, empty parking lot toward the dim side door light, I blindly walked directly into a coiled concertina wire barrier near the center of the lot. I was carefully trying to unsnag my shirt and pants without tearing them, when a .50 caliber machine gun cut loose directly overhead. There was a gun tower on the edge of the runway overlooking the warehouse complex. The tracers streaked about twenty-five feet above my head and traveled to somewhere out in the bay just beyond the shore. That absolutely scared the shit out of me. I shredded my only sports shirt as I escaped from the barbed wire and ran toward the dim porchlight. I pounded on the door for what seemed a long time before John's roommate finally opened it. As I was pounding. I noticed an immobile, two-foot-long, tan artificial lizard mounted on the door frame just below the light. It was situated to appear to be watching the swarming aggregate of insects buzzing around the light. Being a city boy, I absolutely am not a fan of reptiles but was impressed with the fine detail of that ornamental creature. I have no idea what possessed me to touch it, but as I gently wrapped my fingers around its midsection, it seemed to vanish into thin air. I had no idea that lizards could get that large. As I was about to faint, John's roommate finally opened the door and showed me to a guest room where I immediately crashed for the night. As promised, John did drive me back to the hospital orderly room that next morning where I was finally able to sign-in and begin my in-processing....and, by the way, he revealed that the mouthwatering meat was *DOG. YIKES!* I must confess that I did gag a few times. I have always prided myself on being a dog lover.

That was the beginning of a friendship with John that led to future invitations to Bekins parties and pig roasts with my hooch mates. John contracted civilians from the Philippines in his transport operation. Besides their steadfast work ethic, those men were master chefs in the art of barbecue. John hosted regular pig roasts where his workers killed and prepared a pig, then roasted it all afternoon in a pit filled with red hot charcoal covered with a generous heap of banana tree leaves. Sometime in early 1971, John invited my hooch mates and me to join him and a select few civilian contractors (three of whom I believe were employed by Air America) for a special celebration. On a recent cargo trip to Manilla, he had purchased a medium sized refrigerator and had it equipped with a beer tap on its right side. The interior had been modified to hold a half keg of draft beer. Our job was to help him break it in. Through that afternoon and early evening, we succeeded in draining John's inaugural half keg.

JOHN'S CIVILIAN CONTRACT PHILIPPINE WORKERS DID A FANTASTIC
JOB PREPARING AND ROASTING A PIG ALL AFTERNOON IN A PIT
OF RED-HOT COALS COVERED WITH BANANA TREE LEAVES.

BIG CAT AND JOHN AT OUR CHRISTMAS OF 1970 BEKINS PIG ROAST.

John paid me the honor of tapping the first replacement keg. After I proudly tapped that cask, I noticed that John kept staring at the empty one with a puzzled look. He finally disappeared into the kitchen and after a bit of noisy rummaging in there, returned with a double-bladed axe. We were all comfortably titrated on draft beer and seated in a circle around his living room but scrambled for cover when he raised his axe. John began swinging it at the empty aluminum keg. As expected, his blade bounced off the solid metallic container's exterior. He insisted that there was something inside and that he felt it move around as we switched the kegs in the refrigerator. He finally yielded to the insistence of his drunken guests and retired with the axe and keg to his kitchen where he persisted trying to discover what was inside. As the rest of us dedicated our evening to draining that second keg, we were again interrupted by a lull in the axe blows and a loud scream from John. I ran into the kitchen as fast as I could, fully expecting to find a gaping axe wound in one of John's legs. I found him to be intact but somewhat in shock. He had completely cut that keg in half. Inside we viewed the remains of a dead rat including fur and skeleton. One of the Air America guys did not appear too surprised. He explained that San Miguel was brewed in open vats which often got contaminated with dead leaves and insects. He told us that the final step in their brewing process was careful filtration. That information and what I later learned about the formaldehyde content in some Asian beers at the time made me an orthodox consumer of American beers.

John was a very friendly, outgoing, and generous young man. I was grateful for our chance meeting and his friendship. Vietnam was a place where great friends briefly entered our lives, shared memorable times......some happy, some sad, and some dangerous......then quickly disappeared as we each DEROSed (reached our date of expected return from overseas). It was sad that such fast and true friendships faded so quickly upon our return to the real world. A world where we all had to work very hard to fit back in......a world that was now condemning us for having served.

BODY ID

C am Ranh Bay Air Force Base was my first permanent duty
assignment following basic orientation and small arms
training. I had much to learn about Air Force life, Air Force dentistry, and life in a war zone. After I had been in-country for
about a month and had settled into long days of toothaches
and fillings, I discovered that it was my turn to cover the DOD
(Dental Officer of the Day) schedule the following week. That
week-long responsibility was assigned to junior dental officers
on a rotational basis to manage dental emergencies during off
duty hours. These were usually abscessed or broken teeth,
acute gum problems or pericoronitis. That was never an easy
or pleasant assignment.

Early on Sunday morning, I was aroused by the ringing
phone in our hooch. Assuming that it was a dental sick call, I
answered, yawning, "Hello."

The voice on the other end simply said, "Git yer ass over
here, doc, I've got a couple of dead ones for ya." Then he hung

up. Assuming it to be a crank call, I hung up and climbed back into my bunk.

At that point, my hooch mate Big Cat asked, "Meier, who was that?"

After I told him what had been said, he repeated, "You better get your ass over to the hospital morgue for some body ID."

My only thought was...... "What the hell is body ID?"

I had just graduated from dental school a few months earlier. No one had ever told me about a dentist's role in forensic endeavors. Nor was it ever mentioned during my basic Air Force orientation. Following Big Cat's directions, I found the morgue close to the back of our clinic building. It consisted of two small, conjoined cube-like modular buildings. Once I got within twenty-five yards of the door, I could smell the rotting remains of whatever was awaiting me inside. The stench inside was overwhelming. There were two closed body bags lying on the floor. The sergeant in charge explained that the remains inside the bags were those of two young fliers who had gone down into the bush some three weeks earlier. Due to the sweltering tropical temperatures and conditions in the jungle, the remains of these two Air Force Academy graduates had completely deteriorated beyond recognition. My job was to make a definitive identification of each by comparing my dental findings with their official Air Force Dental Records which the sergeant had on site. There was no x-ray unit in the morgue so I could not try to take a radiographic series to compare with the films in their dental records. There was no overhead light to aid intraoral visibility. My only tools were a dental mirror, a denture brush, and a squeeze bottle of water. To add to the difficulty at hand, my assigned dental assistant, who should have recorded my findings on a blank dental chart, was retching so badly that he could not stand to be in the room with the body bags. Consequently, he uselessly kept stepping outside until he finally stayed outside. As a result, I had to do all my own charting as I saw it...tooth by tooth.

The first task was to unzip the body bags. The morgue sergeant and I each quickly learned that both bodies had been placed face down in their respective bag. They were probably rolled in to minimize additional damage to those mutilated corpses. The overwhelming odor made it hard to breath. One victim was still wearing his shoulder holster. Though no weapon was present, some bullets remained in the bandolier over his right shoulder. Approximately half of the .38 caliber rounds had slipped out of the bandolier and were scattered around the body bag. Their badly stained and charred flight suits were crawling with maggots. We had to work together to turn the bodies over. As I tugged on the arm of the flier wearing the shoulder holster, that arm came off in my hands. The body cavity created where the arm had detached poured forth an unbelievable flood of maggots. The faces of both men had been flattened beyond recognition. The deterioration had discolored their skin to where it was impossible to even guess at their race. The only feature that even hinted that these were human remains was a mustache on one of the crushed faces.

The oral cavities of both bodies were packed with rotting debris and maggots. Because of rigor mortis, the shattered jaws were immovable making it impossible to clear the pu-trid dreck with just my fingers and the denture brush. As the morgue sergeant watched me hopelessly trying to manually force the jaws open in an effort to expose the teeth, he finally said, "Doc! What the fuck are you doing?" He then fetched large tin snip-like shears. He used them to cut both cheeks of the first body from the corners of the mouth to the jaw joints. He then produced a long, flat stainless-steel instrument that re-sembled a tire iron. With it he pried the jaws open giving me a direct view of both arches at the same time. He then left it to me to do the same to the second cadaver. I then began vigor-ous scrubbing along with considerable gagging trying to elimi-nate the caked oral detritus. Using only my squeeze-bottle and denture brush, I was able to eliminate enough of the decaying, black soft tissue to allow visualization of the teeth for charting. Since my useless assistant remained outside dealing with his dry heaves, I had to alternate between going nose to nose with the putrescent mouths and a blank dental chart page. Suffice it to say, as a one-man job, the process took much longer than necessary. My task was to record missing and broken teeth as well as all dental restorations. I did get through the second re-cording more efficiently thanks to what I had learned from the first case. After that seemingly endless process, I was able to go outside, breathe some slightly fresher air, and compare my charting with that in the official dental records of both victims. That was the easy part...and a welcome break from the morgue. Once identities had been verified, official papers signed, and the bodies properly tagged with their identities, I was done.

I had not yet eaten that Sunday morning but food was the last thing on my mind. I just wanted to take a shower and incinerate the jungle fatigues that I had been wearing. Before I headed out, I cast a parting glance back at those dead fliers. They were both younger than me. As Air Force Academy graduates, they were both probably brighter than me. They had both forfeited their lives and promising careers for a country that no longer supported them nor appreciated their sacrifice. America at that time had turned against our soldiers who were forced to wage that unpopular war, instead of the politicians who were prolonging it. In the end, my only consolation was that I had helped to ensure that two grieving families at least received their sons' correct remains.

DUST OFF

One of my most indelible memories of Cam Ranh Bay was the incessant chopping of Hueys overhead. The Huey (UH-1 Iroquois) was a multi-purpose helicopter used extensively throughout the Vietnam War. By the late 1960s the B and D models had been introduced. They featured more powerful engines, stronger air frames, and larger cabins enabling them to carry greater capacities. Their range was reported to be about 350 miles and cruising speed at 128 mph (maximum speed approximately 140 mph). Hueys were set up in three different configurations depending on their mission. The Slick was intended to be a troop or supply transport. The term Slick implied that they were not outfitted with protective armaments other than weapons carried by the troops whom they were transporting. Their wide-open doors allowed troops to quickly exit in hostile territory while the chopper hovered just above the ground without touching down. That tactic also enabled the Huey to make a quick departure from the LZ (landing zone).

TYPICAL SLICK TRANSPORTING TROOPS.

Hueys configured as assault gunships were armed with machine guns, rockets, and automatic grenade launchers. The most fearsome of these were equipped with the dreaded 7.62 NATO mini-gun. This was a six barreled, electrical driven weapon that could deliver a rate of fire of either two thousand or six thousand rounds per minute. These Hueys were outfitted with an enormous magazine mounted on the rear wall that spanned the width of the cabin. Their sound while firing was not that of a machine gun but rather a very loud air horn. Though only every fifth round was a tracer bullet, their incredible rate of fire resulted in making the tracers appear as a solid red line like a laser beam.

ASSAULT HELICOPTER MAINTENANCE AT CAM RANH BAY IN 1971.

ASSAULT HELICOPTER OUTFITTED WITH A MINI-GUN.

MINI-GUN MOUNTED ON A HUEY GUN SHIP.

HUEY GUNSHIP TAKING OFF FOR EVENING PATROL
AT CAM RANH BAY AFB IN 1971.

Hueys intended to be air ambulances to transport wounded from active combat sites to a rear medical facility were known as Dust Offs. The courageous and rapid action of those medevac helicopter crews braving hot LZs (landing zones under fire) to evacuate casualties resulted in reducing the mortality rate of the wounded to less than 2 percent. Early on during the war, the medevac Hueys were unarmed and identified with a large red cross on either side. They soon became priority targets for the enemy. Later in the war, the Dust Offs were crewed with a door gunner. In addition, those venturing into hot LZs often found themselves accompanied by a gunship.

The 483rd USAF hospital at Cam Ranh Bay consisted of multiple buildings. The dental clinic to which I was assigned was a separate building adjacent to the hospital emergency room.

About twenty yards behind the emergency room was a landing pad for helicopters. I witnessed my first Dust Off landing there just a few weeks after my arrival. My hooch mate, Big Cat, and I were approaching the backdoor of our clinic as a Huey touched down. I was not sure what was happening. Four or five emergency technicians had run out with a couple of stretchers as the chopper landed. They immediately placed two badly wounded grunts on the stretchers and ran with them into the emergency room. Next an ER technician slowly escorted three walking wounded wearing blood-stained field bandages. By then the original four stretcher bearers returned to pick up and carry two body bags. As the helicopter idled a bit longer before taking off, one last med-tech returned for a smaller body bag. Big Cat later explained to me that the last bag to leave the chopper cabin usually contained detached body parts, such as arms and legs.

TYPICAL MEDEVAC (DUST OFF) HUEY.

Most of the Dust Off pilots whom I met during my tour were very young and fearless US Army warrant officers. In the end, they were the war heroes whom I most respected. Without hesitation, they flew into active combat sectors, often without armament, and were sitting ducks as they evacuated the wounded.

MEDCAP

Just a few months after I had matriculated at The University of Pittsburgh's School of Dental Medicine, I received a draft notice and was ordered to report for my Selective Service physical examination. It was 1966. The Vietnam War was raging and Congress had just placed a limit of four years on the full-time student draft exemption. Prior to that time, "draft dodgers" could avoid military service by delaying graduation but continuously registering as full-time students. This practice of becoming a "professional student" was expensive and certainly favored sons of the wealthy. The other route followed by those escaping military service obligations was to defect and head for countries like Canada. Unfortunately, the 1966 Draft Law revision put many medical and dental students in jeopardy of having their training interrupted. The law was again amended in 1967 to correct that oversite by extending the "2-S" exemption to allow health professions students the necessary time to complete their programs. However, that interim year without the health professions exemption created a multiplicity of problems for those of us who were in training at that time. Since I had a high draft lottery number, there was a delay of a few months before I would have been "sworn-in" and placed on active duty. Shortly after my induction physical examination, I discovered the existence of Army, Navy, and Air Force Medical Inactive Reserve Units. Acceptable student candidates were sworn-in as lieutenants and hence were no longer eligible for the draft. There were no scholarships, uniforms, or pay checks for inactive reserve members, but they were protected from education interruptions until their schooling had been completed. Upon graduation, members of those reserve units were very quickly assigned to active duty to fulfill two-year commitments to their respective service. By the time I had learned about those detachments, the Army and Navy Programs had been filled. However, I did manage to get an offer from the US Air Force.

Around the middle of my senior year, our reserve units queried us to submit our top three choices for assignment. While my classmates jockeyed for bases in places like Hawaii, Florida, or somewhere in Western Europe, I requested Vietnam at a time when the war had become very unpopular. Most of my classmates thought that I was insane. That was late 1969. Most of my life-long friends had already served in Southeast Asia as enlisted men. A cousin had been killed there. My intention in volunteering was not to fight the war as a grunt but to serve by taking care of our warriors. I also wanted very much to participate in MEDCAP (Medical Civic Action Program) efforts which rendered care to Vietnamese civilians trying to survive in rural hamlets in the midst of that war. No medical or dental services were available throughout the Vietnamese countryside. The My Lai massacre that had occurred in 1968 had a profound impact on me. That incident compelled me to volunteer for an assignment where I could render some kind of meaningful help to such unfortunate villagers.

The Air Force was more than happy to accommodate my assignment request. Rather than assigning me to Vietnam during the second year of my obligation, after I had been introduced and accommodated to military life, they sent me to Cam Ranh Bay Air Force Base directly after my graduation from dental school. My lack of understanding of military protocol created situations for me in Vietnam that ultimately provided material for this series of memoirs.

I was assigned to the 483rd USAF hospital which was the largest US military hospital outside the United States. Its 475 beds were distributed throughout well sandbagged Quonset hut wards interconnected by exterior covered walkways. The dental clinic was usually manned by ten dentists (one from the Navy) and fourteen enlisted personnel (including two from the Navy). We junior officers, all captains (dai-uys), were general dentists. The clinic commander was a colonel. The other three senior officers included a prosthodontist, an oral surgeon, and a periodontist (all lieutenant colonels). Our patients came from all four branches of the military. We junior officers worked ten-hour days, six days per week filling teeth and relieving dental pain. Each week one or two dentists and their assistants travelled from the base to a village on the western shore of Cam Ranh Bay for a MEDCAP mission.

483RD USAF HOSPITAL DENTAL CLINIC AT CAM
RANH BAY AFB, VIETNAM IN 1970.

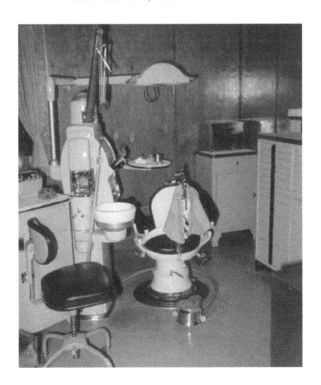

MY VERY FIRST DENTAL OPERATORY FOLLOWING
DENTAL SCHOOL GRADUATION.

These missions were voluntary. All dentists did not participate. Only three of us rotated regularly for these missions and usually completed one or two missions per month (security conditions permitting). Occasionally others came along to help. Approximately half of my missions were only manned by one dental assistant and myself. The expectation was for us to extract as many abscessed teeth as possible during our allotted time in the field. Transportation for these trips was provided by a beat-up old Dodge crackerbox ambulance. The only time that I drove that hulk was during my first mission. Negotiating the notorious Highway 1 traffic that single time was enough for me.

WELL-WORN DODGE CRACKERBOX THAT PROVIDED
OUR MEDCAP TRANSPORTATION.

TYPICAL HIGHWAY 1 SCENES.

TYPICAL HIGHWAY 1 TRAFFIC.

Highway 1 did not seem to have a right side of the road. Vespa scooters and three-wheeled taxies weaved in and out of ox-carts, sheep and goose herders, pedestrians, and military vehicles. I made my assistant drive on all subsequent missions while I rode shotgun. We completed all our missions on the mainland side of Cam Ranh Bay, in the marketplace of Ba Ngoi (also known as Cam Lam, shown on the map below). There was a concrete block dispensary in the market place that contained a dental treatment room.

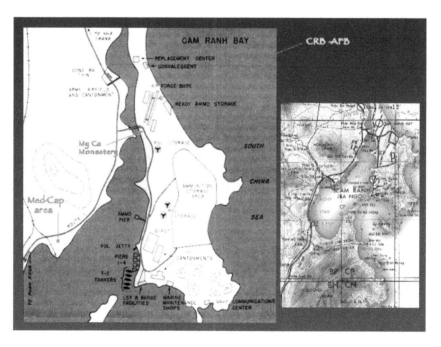

MEDCAP MISSIONS WERE CONDUCTED AT THE VILLAGE OF BA NGOI.

TYPICAL STREET SCENES IN THE BA NGOI MARKET PLACE.

The room was equipped with two modern dental units and chairs but had no electricity. Consequently, nothing worked. We had no lights. We had no radiographs. We only had a nonadjustable chair for the patients to sit in. On most days the tropical heat and humidity there were suffocating. Septic conditions surrounded us not only in the adjacent market place, but also within our small structure. One week as we were entering the building and about to set up, we noticed a disgusting putrid mess of afterbirth on a stainless-steel table in the next room. One wall of the dental treatment room had large shutters that opened into the market place. An audience usually gathered to peer in and wait to hear the moans of patients for whom we could not achieve adequate local anesthesia. That was not unusual in cases of severe abscesses where huge amounts of pus and inflammation were present. When someone did moan or scream, we would often hear cheers coming from the crowd. There was a little girl who always seemed to be in our extraction audience. She was always alone and always smiling. I eventually got the idea that she may have been a bi-racial orphan who was cared for by some of the marketplace vendors. I took her picture once. If there could have been a way possible, I would have adopted her. Her impact on me eventually led me to adopt a bi-racial child some years later. But that story is the subject of another memoir. The people always knew that we only came on Tuesdays. By the time we arrived, a very, very long line of patients seeking extractions would have already formed. For security reasons, we had to meet a curfew upon returning to our base. There were weeks when we were not able to accommodate all the waiting patients. More than half of our patients required incision and drainage of incredibly large abscesses that could not adequately drain following extraction of the offending tooth. I still clearly remember one particular patient, a middle-aged lieutenant colonel assigned to the South Vietnamese army. Teeth numbers eighteen and nineteen were badly broken down and abscessed. His left cheek was swollen to the size of a baseball. Local anesthesia failed due to all the infection present. Unfortunately, there was little to no drainage from the extraction sites. When I incised into the swollen facial vestibule adjacent to the extraction sites, there was an explosion of blood and pus that gushed out onto my arm, face, and fatigue blouse. The patient felt immediate relief for which he was grateful. However, I just wanted to take a shower and burn my uniform. We only had aspirin to pass out for pain. We had no antibiotics. Our situation and equipment in the bush were primitive to say the least. We did have local anesthesia and disposable needles. But we only had one, sometimes two complete trays of oral surgery instruments. We carried about two or three gallons of zephiran chloride solution and a large dishpan so that we could quickly rinse the blood and tissue from our instruments between patients. By the end of the day, it looked like a pan of very muddy water.

MEMBERS OF OUR EXODONTIA AUDIENCE.

We each had a pair or two of surgical gloves but after two or three patients the gloves developed holes and began to leak. We soon had to abandon them and perform most of the extractions barehanded. Most patients would only allow us to extract one tooth. I remember one such elderly mama-san with badly blackened betel nut teeth. They were so periodontally involved that they seemed to move when she spoke. I saw her every time that I went out there. I felt like we knew each other. By the time I left Vietnam, my MEDCAP colleagues and I had only succeeded in clearing all her maxillary teeth. Her mandibular teeth still needed to go.

Before departing on a MEDCAPmission, we were temporarily issued weapons by our orderly room. Dental officers were issued a .38 caliber Smith and Wesson model 15 revolver along with twelve bullets. The dental assistant was issued a standard .223 caliber Colt M-16 rifle along with two twenty round magazines, certainly not much with which to defend ourselves. However, no one ever seemed to shoot at us because we actually treated many VC (Viet Cong) patients on those missions.

PACKED UP AND READY TO HEAD BACK TO THE BASE AFTER A VERY LONG DAY OF EXTRACTIONS AT BA NGOI. I WAS ARMED WITH MY ISSUED .38 CALIBER REVOLVER AND WAS ALSO HOLDING MY ASSISTANTS M-16 RIFLE.

SMITH AND WESSON .38 CALIBER MODEL-15 REVOLVER.

VIETNAM ERA COLT .223 CALIBER M-16 RIFLE.

Part of the military's MEDCAP purpose was to win the hearts and minds of the people with such efforts. Prior to leaving for my third mission, I reported to the orderly room for a revolver issue. I was informed that none were available because most of the hospital physicians had checked them all out prior to attending a medical symposeum in Saigon for the next few days. The sergeant in charge produced his only handgun, which was useless. It was a model-15 that was so rusted that the cylinder barely turned. In addition, both wooden grips were missing. I thought that he was joking. Unfortunately, he was not. He did however, issue me an M-16 for the day.

Hospital personel were not permitted to keep any personal weapons. As one of the few hospital officers who regulary volunteered for MEDCAP duty, I was determined to be able to defend myself should we ever run into trouble on these weekly excursions of mercy into the bush. For whatever reasons, only our hospital's dentists carried out scheduled MEDCAP missions to villages around Cam Ranh Bay. I was not aware of our physicians going out there on a regular basis. We unfortunately had a hospital commander who had little to no regard for dentists. He arrived there shortly before me. During my tour, he had been known to downgrade and cancel end of tour medals for a number of our dental personel. It seemed that dentists were second class citizens at our hospital despite our contrbutions.

Imprudently, I decided to take care of myself on my missions to the coutryside by purchasing my own weapon on the black market. Prior to entering active duty, I had competed in a local Pittsburgh police pistol league. I was very familiar with the Colt government model-1911 .45 automatic pistol and had experienced a few years of competition with it. As chance would have it, I had a patient who was a hospital supply sergeant on his second tour in Vietnam. He had a reputation for having assembled a widespread, unofficial network based on trading and selling goods and services. I approached him after a dental appointment and inquired about the purchase of a servicable .45 automatic pistol and a small amount of ammo that could accompany me on MEDCAP missions. Three days later, he arrived at my hooch with a GI ammo can.

WWII VINTAGE REMINGTON RAND .45 AUTO PISTOL WITH SHOULDER HOLSTER RIG THAT I MADE AT THE BASE HOBBY SHOP AT CAM RANH BAY AIR FORCE BASE IN 1971.

Inside was a WWII vintage Remington Rand .45 auto pistol resting on about half a can of loose hardball ammo. The gun was in remarkable condition. He charged me twenty-five dollars for the lot. There was a small hobby shop on the base intended to give off-duty troops something to do besides drink alcohol or smoke contraband weed. Inside was a corner devoted to simple ceramic work. I did make myself a beer mug there which I still have. Another corner housed a lapidary section where I learned to polish semiprecious stones and place them in cheap settings for my wife and mother. In addition, there was a small leather shop in another corner. That was where I fabricated a shoulder holster rig for my newly acquired pistol. Skinny as I was back then, I could wear my rig and pistol beneath my jungle fatigue blouse without attracting any attention. Only my hooch mates knew. I carried that piece on all of my remaining missions. When it came time to leave Vietnam, I realized that the customs inspectors would find and confiscate it. So, I sold it for twenty-six dollars to a major friend of mine who happened to be assigned to base supply.

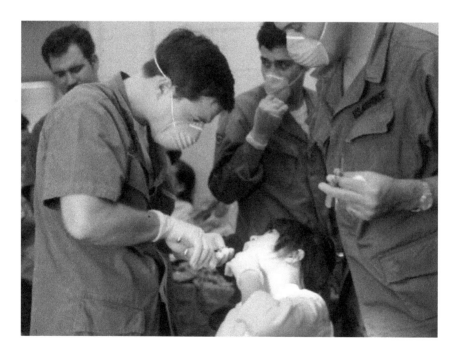

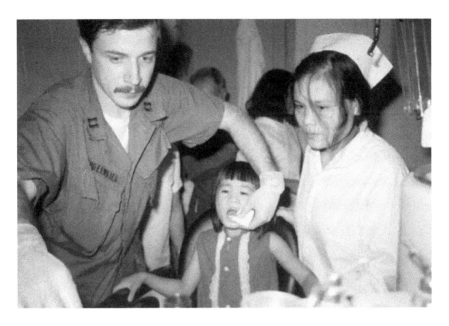

A VERY HOT AND HUMID DAY PULLING LOTS
OF TEETH IN THE MARKET PLACE.

My most indelible MEDCAP memory occurred during one of
my last trips to Ba Ngoi. It was particularly hot and humid that
day. I was accompanied by two dental assistants and our base
periodontist. Though I was not aware of him ever accompany-
ing any of us before on these missions, he was definitely a huge
help that day. It was exhausting, but we actually did treat everyone in our long waiting line. As we were packing up our gear
into the old ambulance, a small group of locals approached
carrying a young girl on a stretcher. All were speaking excit-
edly and at once in Vietnamese. I did not understand the language but I did recognize one word. That word was *bac-si*,
the Vietnamese word for doctor. In that culture there was no

distinction between a physician, a dentist, or a veterinarian...a doctor was a doctor. They absolutely did not understand that I was a dentist and not a physician. There was a nurse who was stationed at our market place dispensary who spoke almost no English. The girl on the stretcher was covered with a sheet all the way up to her chin. Her stretcher was resting on the filthy ground of the market place. From the expression on her face, it was obvious that she was suffering from considerable pain. In the midst of all this confusion, someone pulled off her sheet exposing her nude body to the market place crowd. I kept trying to cover her, but her mother kept pulling down the sheet and pointing to her left hip. I finally gathered from the nurse that she was twelve years old and had broken that hip some time ago. It seemed to be healing until she fell recently and apparently fractured it again. We were under strict orders to never bring any of our MEDCAP patients back to the base. Besides the well-guarded check point at the main gate of our base there was a heavily guarded check point at the bridge that connected Cam Ranh peninsula to the mainland. All Vietnamese nationals employed at one of the large bases on the peninsula had to pass through those check points and be thoroughly searched each day as they went to and from their jobs. Absolutely no locals were permitted to remain on the peninsula after curfew.

As I was trying to figure out a way to help that child, another woman stepped out of that discombobulated crowd carrying a baby that was about a year and a half old. His neck was so swollen that he could not move his head. He was in respiratory distress and could not even cry. He looked just like the cellulitis photos in my head and neck pathology book. There was a dark brown sticky-fluid leaking out from under four band-aids that had been placed on his neck. Our periodontist carefully peeled one off only to find that there was no open abscess underneath. We later found out that this was a folk medicine attempt at a cure. The brown fluid smeared under the band-aids was an herbal mixture containing fecal material. I was convinced that he probably would not survive another twenty-four hours.

At that point I was determined to do whatever I could for those kids. I informed Bernie, our periodontist, that we were going to take both children back to our hospital. He absolutely refused, insisting that we had to respect the standing order to not bring any indigenous patients back from our missions. He certainly outranked me but it was my mission and he came along as a guest and helper. Besides, I did have a Pittsburgh West End personality that was a bit stronger than his. We loaded both children and their mothers with our periodontist and his assistant into the back of the crackerbox. My assistant drove and I rode shotgun. We kept the young girl on her stretcher in the center of the ambulance floor. The first obstacle was to get past Check-Point Charlie at the bridge to the peninsula. As we left the marketplace, I went for broke and turned on the rotating red light atop the ambulance.

As we approached the bridge, the busy guards never stopped us. They simply waved us through. The last obstacle was the main gate at Cam Ranh Bay Air Force Base. My assistant nervously asked me, "Doc, what the fuck are we going to do now?" I was committed. I leaned over and turned on our siren. I had no idea if it was even operational. Well, it worked, loud and clear. I told my assistant to slow down but not to stop. Miraculously we made it. Those gate guards also waved us through. We drove straight to our hospital's emergency room. We were fortunate to arrive on a day when they were not flooded with emergencies or war casualties. My assistant backed our vehicle up to the unloading pad as several emergency room technicians ran out to meet us. When they opened the ambulance back doors, they exposed our nervous periodontist, the two desperate foreign national mothers, and our stretcher patient.

CHECK-POINT CHARLIE WAS ON THE MAINLAND SIDE OF THE BRIDGE.

CAM RANH BAY AIR FORCE BASE MAIN GATE 1971.

Everyone was talking...no, yelling all at once. Since my job was done, I elected to quietly open my door, slip out, and slowly walk away...as one would expect, I kept a very low profile for the remainder of that week. I had no communication with our periodontist or clinic commander. I also heard nothing about the fate of the two kids whom I had driven back to the base. Finally, I queried a young general medical officer (GMO) and friend who lived in the hooch next to mine. He informed me that we apparently had picked the right time for our daring rescue. Not much else was happening at the hospital that day. I learned that our physicians had apparently saved the lives of both of my unauthorized passengers. Remarkably, no one in my chain of command ever mentioned the event to me.

I was very fortunate to have received that assignment to Cam Ranh Bay. Though many rockets had been fired at us during those days and nights, none hit our hooch or hospital. I made a few life-long friends there, all of whom escaped injury. Most of all, I am very grateful that I was able to accomplish what had originally prompted me to volunteer. I rendered general dental care to hundreds of our GIs who had to fight that unpopular war. In addition, I was able to deliver some help to locals in the field on my MEDCAP missions. I never performed any heroic acts, never shot anyone, or saved anyone's life. But I do take satisfaction in the fact that I enabled our hospital docs to save the lives of two children because I once gave them a ride.

DENTISTRY GONE TO THE DOGS

THE BEACHCOMBER, CAM RANH BAY AFB, VIETNAM 1971.

Late one steamy afternoon, after a long day treating decaying teeth and bleeding gums, I returned home to the Beachcomber. There I found my hooch-mate, Vic extremely bummed over a disagreement that he had experienced with his supervisor earlier that day. Vic was the junior veterinarian assigned to the 483rd USAF Hospital at that time. His boss intended to euthanize one of the sentry dogs that had recently lost thirteen pounds and would no longer bite during attack training. The major's diagnosis was kidney failure. But Vic, a captain, insisted that Rex was suffering from gastritis secondary to severe dental problems. Vic asked me if I would look at Old Rex. In true MASH fashion (which is how everything seemed to work at the 483rd Hospital) I, of course, answered yes.

Veterinary dentistry was essentially unheard of in 1971. The only solution for animal dental problems in the past had been the crude extraction of the offending teeth. In the case of security dogs, extraction of certain key teeth, like the canines, would make the dog ineffective and usually led to its being put down.

As it turned out, I was the dental officer on duty (DOD) that week and the only one who would potentially be in the dental clinic that Sunday. Further enabling our mission for Rex was the fact that our commanding officer used to catch hops to Saigon via the Friday afternoon milk runs. He never returned from those weekly R&Rs until late in the day on Mondays. So…it seemed that the clinic was ours for the weekend. Having grown up in Pittsburgh's West End, I learned at an early age that asking for forgiveness after the fact usually yielded better results than asking for permission ahead of time only to be denied. Rather than seeking the colonel's permission, Vic and I covertly prepared for the brave sentry dog's first dental appointment. On Sunday morning, while Vic transported his gas machine from the vet clinic (to sedate Rex), I replaced the dental chair in my operatory with a gurney that I had commandeered from the hospital emergency room next door to the dental clinic. Rex and his weary handler showed up around midmorning.

REX AND HIS HANDLER.

Rex was placed under general anesthesia and kept there for over three hours that day. Even though we had locked both clinic doors to assure security for this clandestine operation, everyone and their grandmother seemed to show up for a peek and of course to take pictures. There was no way to keep this quiet.

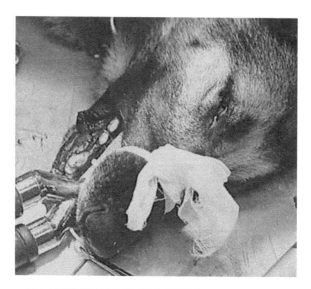

VIC ASSURED PROFOUND ANESTHESIA BEFORE I
DARED APPROACH MY FOUR-LEGGED PATIENT

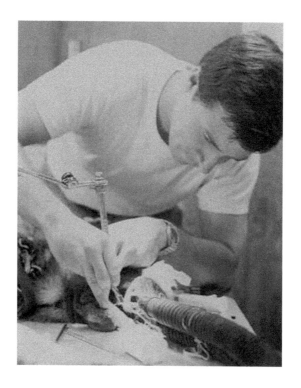

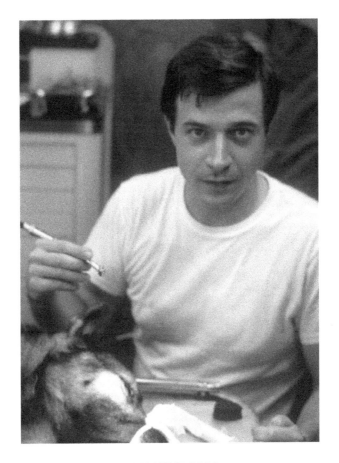

DOG? WHAT DOG?

Examination revealed that our patient had fractured both of his lower canines and had exposed their pulps. These dogs often aggressively attacked their chain-link kennel enclosures when strangers approached. In addition, he had a carious pulp exposure of his lower right tricuspid tooth, the largest tooth in a dog's mandible. Since this was a pre-veterinary dentistry period, the only way that I could imagine treating Rex was the same way that I would have treated his two-legged security police handlers. My treatment plan was to complete root canal fillings on the two fractured lower canines followed by two cast post and core gold crowns. I saw no way to save the abscessed tricuspid, so I decided to extract it. The root canals were huge. Were it not for a box of unused, extremely long anterior endodontic files that we found in the supply room; I could not have reached the canine apices. Once adequate filing had been completed, I plugged about five pounds of gutta percha into those enormous canals. At that point, I was able to finalize preparation of the teeth to receive the cast gold restorations.

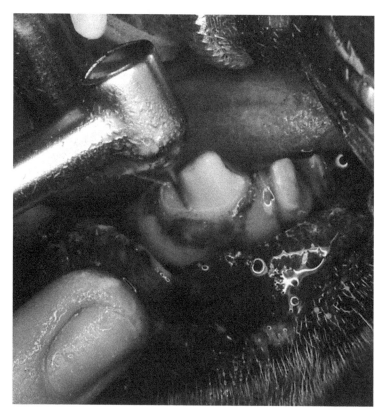

CROWN PREPARATION.

Following final impressions, there was no practical way to fabricate temporary coverage for the two crown preparations. Since Rex had been suspended from strike training and had been placed on a controlled diet, I decided to gamble and forgo any temporary crowns. I protected the root canal fillings with temporary gutta percha stopping and simply crossed my fingers that he would not somehow damage the tooth preparations while the definitive crowns were being fabricated. After having made final impressions, I then had to face the most difficult extraction of my career. I quickly learned how strong a dog's mandibular bone is. It seemed to totally consist of stone like cortical bone. As I began sectioning the tooth to facilitate easier removal, Rex yawned. Needless to say, I cleared the deck by at least three feet. Because I had been taught to absolutely remove all root fragments, I was determined to assure that for Rex. That extraction did require considerable tooth sectioning and bone reduction, but I finally succeeded. After I had placed a couple of resorbable sutures, we had finished. It was only after we had transported Rex back to the kennels that Vic asked why I had spent so much time trimming and smoothing bone and carefully removing any and all root fragments. Only then did he say, "Why didn't you just break the teeth off like we vets do and leave the roots there?" I then had to ask him, "Why the hell didn't you tell me that a couple of hours ago?"

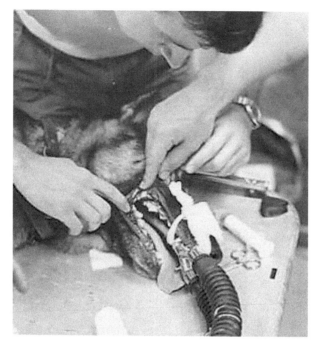

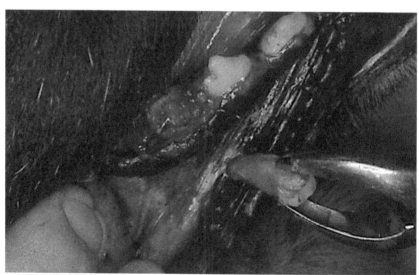

SECTIONED RIGHT LOWER TRICUSPID REMOVAL...
FAR TOUGHER THAN ANTICIPATED.

I waxed-up the restorations myself during the following few evenings when the clinic was closed. I had found a dog anatomy book in the hospital library which was a big help. My greatest dilemma came when it was time to cast the crowns. It had never occurred to me to use anything other than type III gold to fabricate those crowns. Afterall, that was how I was trained and how I treated my two-legged patients. Joe, our clinic's dental laboratory technician absolutely refused to have anything to do with Rex's case! I assured him that I had already completed the wax-ups and would be happy to invest, cast, and finish the restorations myself if he would just issue me the gold. Though the price of gold in 1971 was nowhere near what it is today, it was still very valuable and strict records were kept to account for its use. Joe did finally agree to issue enough type III gold to fabricate the two massive restorations. However, to cover his ass he insisted on a properly completed and signed laboratory form requesting the alloy. Without hesitation, I completed the AF form 513. Rex, as all other security dogs, had a service number, so I used that. I gave him the rank of airman first class, and finally the name of Rex Harrison. Then I boldly signed it. I completed the casting and polishing that very night. The following Sunday, while our colonel was again sampling the Saigon culture, we met in our dental clinic for Rex's crown delivery appointment. After he had reached an adequate level of anesthesia, I observed that his extraction site was healing very well. Vic then gave me the good news that Rex had regained nearly all his lost weight and would soon return to training and duty.

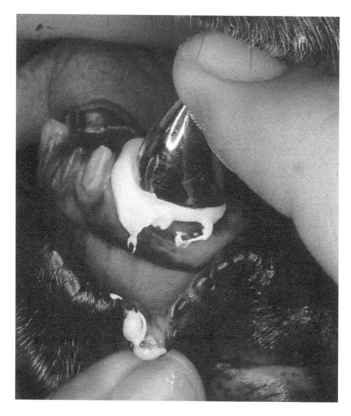

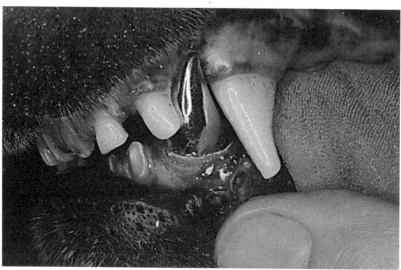

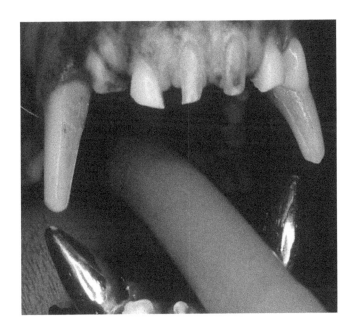

CROWN DELIVERY WITH ZINC PHOSPHATE CEMENT.

After some minor adjustments the crowns were cemented into place with zinc phosphate cement. Rex was revived and returned to his kennel to sleep off the after effects of the anesthesia.

REX SLEEPING OFF THE EFFECTS OF HIS ANESTHESIA

POST DELIVERY CROWN RETENTION CHECK.

I thought that was that. It was a good story and I had plenty of pictures to prove it. However, I was one naive young captain to think that I could make two and a half ounces of government gold disappear from a military clinic unnoticed. Approximately two weeks after Rex had returned to duty, I was summoned to the colonel's office. Was he ever pissed! He chewed my ass up one wall then down another. That day, the colonel added a new word to my vocabulary, Leavenworth! The only thing that saved me was the fact that old Rex had been spared from his planned euthanasia and had returned to duty. Consequently, there would be no Leavenworth. But because of my unconventional acquisition methods, there also would not be any commendation for saving such a valuable Air Force asset. Whew! Needless to say, that was one of the major reasons why I left Vietnam with no recognition medals other than the service medal for simply having served there.

Because of Rex, I found some great friends among the boys on K-9 hill. Though they were the courageous troops who kept us safe at night, we day-timers rarely saw them. They had to get their sleep during the day. Rex really looked cool with his two gold teeth. The handlers promised to send me one of those teeth when Old Rex finally went on to meet his Maker. I left Cam Ranh Bay in the early Summer of 1971 but never did get my gold tooth. That was probably because of an outrageous decision made by our government at the end of the Vietnam conflict. It was decided to not bring back any of the military sentry or patrol dogs. All were put down in Vietnam. Their handlers were required to hold them in their arms as the needles were inserted and they slowly expired. Besides such an inexcusable extermination of those brave K9s, the anguish that this action heaped upon their handlers plagued many of them for years. Following an outcry from handlers and civilians alike, rules were later put in place to prevent such an atrocity from ever happening again. Such dogs can now be rescued by properly selected and trained individuals, many of whom had formerly been security dog handlers.

A ROUGH FLIGHT

The holiday season of 1970 was a lonely one. I spent it in my Cam Ranh Bay hooch with my two bunk mates, Dave "Big Cat" Van Tasell and Art "Lo-ball" Kobal, and close friend Bob Moles. My holiday seasons up until then had been very happy times spent at home with members of both sides of my family. Throughout my childhood, Dad would devote many weeks leading up to Christmas in a screened-off section in our basement setting up a Lionel train display. My mother, grandmother, and other ladies of our clan spent days baking Christmas cookies and German Kuchen...my favorite. My closest friends and I served as choir boys at St Martin's church in Pittsburgh's West End where we rehearsed our holiday repertoire for weeks on end. All the while, my younger sisters and I went to sleep at night speculating on what Santa would bring us. But that Christmas of 1970 was destined to be a sad one. It was the first one without Dad, who had died suddenly of a massive heart attack a just few months earlier. I was sent to Vietnam just one month after his death. My reporting date to Vietnam had been delayed for several weeks as a humanitarian consideration to help my mother deal with arrangements following Dad's untimely passing. However, I did have to meet the not later than reporting date in my assignment orders to Cam Ranh Bay. To further complicate matters, my first-born son, Lee was due just before my deployment. Despite the extension of my reporting date, Lee apparently had decided to arrive late. He was born exactly three weeks after I had arrived in country. News of his birth marked that day as the happiest of my adult life up to that point. I bought a box of cigars and candy bars to pass out to everyone I saw to celebrate that special day. Little did I know that Lee's mother was about to descend into a postpartum depression from which she would never completely recover.

Because of the delay and unreliability of our mail, I had asked members of my family to refrain from sending me any holiday presents or treats that year. Cookies, if they arrived at all were usually crumbled and stale. Much to my surprise, my wife sent me a telegram shortly before Thanksgiving. Expecting a seasonal greeting, I sat down and anxiously opened my unexpected wire. That terse message from my wife of three and a half years contained only two sentences, *"I want out! The baby is with your sister."* To this day, that has been the only telegram that I have ever received. My three friends (actually, my "in country" brothers) sat me down, titrated me with generous amounts of Kentucky bourbon, and helped me formulate a plan to get back home to address this unimaginable situation. We soon discovered that I had to apply for emergency leave through the American Red Cross office at our hospital. Their protocol was to investigate and verify the legitimacy of an emergency via their stateside offices before approving such a leave request from the war zone. That process took a number of days. The bastard who ran our Red Cross office at Cam Ranh Bay reacted toward me with a very put-off attitude. He dealt with me as though I were lying in order to get reassigned (even though I had volunteered for my assignment to Vietnam). Since the Red Cross Representative in Pittsburgh was unable to carry on much of a conversation with my uncooperative wife, they did not approve an emergency leave. Instead, I was granted two weeks of humanitarian leave.

PICTURE TAKEN BY BIG CAT OF ME SITTING ON OUR HOOCH REVETMENT AFTER RECEIVING WORD OF LEE'S ARRIVAL.

That meant that I had to travel Space A (space available). In effect, that reduced my actual leave time in Pittsburgh due to the inevitable waiting time for available space on the essential flights. In addition, I was required to return to Vietnam in order to apply for a humanitarian reassignment. Had I been granted an emergency leave; I could have applied for humanitarian re-assignment while back home attending to my problems. This requirement to return to Vietnam also increased my required travel time. In short, I was granted a two-week humanitarian leave but only about five days were available to attend to my problems at home.

I slept through nearly the entire trip from Cam Ranh Bay Air Force Base to the Seattle-Tacoma Air Port. Just before I boarded the Freedom Bird filled with troops finally going home, Big Cat gave me a phenobarbital capsule to enable me to sleep. I slept soundly through the first refueling stop at Tachikawa Air Force Base in Japan. I woke up briefly to relieve my about to burst bladder when we stopped to refuel at Anchorage, Alaska. I had slept through all the in-flight meals. I was starving by the time we landed at the Seattle-Tacoma International Air Port. I had not eaten in well over twenty-four hours. Since it was some time in the middle of the night, virtually everything in the airport concourse was closed except for one small bar. The only person inside was a young bartender. No food was avail-able except for a few bowls of pretzels scattered around the bar. In my haste to get back home, I did not have a chance to exchange my MPCs for American dollars. Consequently, I had no money. While we were stationed in Vietnam, we were not allowed to possess any American money (greenbacks). We had to exchange any and all American bills and change for military payment certificates (MPCs) which resembled Monopoly game money. MPCs consisted of paper bills in denominations ranging from twenty dollars down to five cents. Without me asking, that bartender generously gave me a beer on the house.

MILITARY PAYMENT CERTIFICATES RANGED IN DENOMINATION FROM FIVE CENTS TO TWENTY DOLLARS.

VIETNAMESE DONG COINS AND PIASTER BILLS HAD TO BE USED INSTEAD OF MPCS WHEN PURCHASING VIETNAMESE GOODS AND SERVICES.

As I munched on pretzels and sipped that bottle of beer, a huge, strapping African-American dude carrying a gigantic boom-box on his left shoulder and wearing a floppy Ivy League style hat entered the deserted bar. He chose to sit on the bar stool immediately to my right. This enormous guy looked like he could have been a pro football lineman. He surmised from my summer uniform (Air Force tan 1505s), no coat and tropical sun tan that I was returning from Vietnam. He informed me that he had served two tours of duty with the Fifth Special Forces (Green Berets) at Dong Ba Thin which was across Cam Ranh Bay just north of our Air Force Base on the peninsula. What a small world. My hospital of assignment provided the medical and dental care for those exceptional soldiers. I had currently been treating two of them. He then insisted on buying my next couple of beers. As we sat there exchanging war stories, an incredibly drunk airline pilot staggered into the bar. His hat was missing. He sported confetti in his hair and was dragging the remains of some streamers around one ankle. Of course, he decided to sit on the barstool to my left. Our conversation soon revealed that he had piloted Air Force C-123 transport planes in Vietnam. The next thing that I knew, he was supplying us with drinks in whiskey glasses. Somewhere during that first round of his purchased drinks, my mind blanked out. Though I had experienced cloudy recollections of drunken episodes in the past, I had never experienced a complete blackout before. At some point, the bartender and my Green Beret brother revived me to a state of semiconsciousness and informed me that my flight to Chicago would soon be leaving. My only memory of that awakening was viewing an incredible collection of empty beer bottles and whiskey glasses littering the bar. My special forces guardian angel accompanied me to the gate and actually helped me onto the plane. A stewardess then strapped me into my seat. I apparently passed out before we left the ground. My mind was a complete blank throughout that flight from the west coast to the windy city. I have utterly no memory of landing, exiting the plane or where I went in the Chicago terminal.

In those days, public restrooms in places like airports were usually outfitted with a row of commodes in locked partitioned stalls. They had coin (dime) operated locks like those found on candy or bubblegum machines. Typically, there was one free toilet at the end of the row for folks who had no change. Since I was unable to exchange my MPCs prior to making that trip, I had no spendable money, including dimes. All the alcohol that I had consumed that night had been purchased by someone else.

TYPICAL GOVERNMENT-CHARTERED SUPER DC-8
FOR VIETNAM WAR TROOP TRANSPORT.

As my bleary mind began to clear, I found myself sitting on a free commode at the end of a row of pay toilets as I was barfing into my pants. I then passed out. There was a large frosted glass window in the wall to my left. While I was vomiting, I noticed that it was dark outside. I have no idea how long I was unconscious. When I regained consciousness, I was still sitting on that same pot now dry-heaving into my pants. I carefully slipped out of my underwear and disposed of them in a waste basket. Fortunately, no one else was in that restroom with me.

By then, the early morning sun had begun to shine through that large frosted window. I did my best to clean myself up with paper towels and water from a sink. I absolutely could not sober up. I had no idea of the time or my whereabouts. My only carry-on item was a large camera case with extra lenses and filters. Remarkably it was all still intact and in my possession. Late during the Vietnam Era, there were usually plenty of military police patrolling the airports looking for out-of-line GIs. I had enough wits about me to understand how much they would have loved to have busted a drunken captain. Before I left that lavatory, I peeked out of the door to see if the coast was clear. I was relieved to see a United Airlines counter directly across the hall from the men's room. Fortunately, there was no waiting line at that counter. As I tried my best to cross that hallway without staggering, the attendant at the counter began to snicker at the sight of me. I had a bit of a problem speaking coherently. So, I simply handed him my ticket. He smiled as he informed me that I had missed two flights from Chicago to Pittsburgh. He did, however find me a seat on an Allegheny Airlines flight that was scheduled to depart in about ten minutes. He quickly switched my ticket and considerately walked me down to the proper gate. Another kind stewardess seated me and fastened my seatbelt. A young man seated to my right introduced himself as a graduate student at the University of Pittsburgh, my alma mater. He was returning from a family visit to Chicago. He insisted on buying me a drink because "as long as people like me were serving in Vietnam, he would not have to go." Thinking that I had to somehow get something nourishing into my inebriated body, I ordered a bloody Mary, hoping that the tomato juice would help. That was another poor decision. I have only scant memories of that flight. As soon as we were airborne, I headed to the toilet to again relieve my bladder and to try to clean up a little better. Upon exiting the lavatory, the two stewardesses who were seated back there went out of their way to accommodate me. I spent the entire flight talking to those beauties, drinking Coca-Cola, and eating whatever snacks they provided. I have no idea what we talked about. They finally got me reseated during final approach. We deplaned down a movable stairway and walked across the tarmac toward a small crowd awaiting passengers just outside the terminal doors. It was early evening on a heavily overcast day. A cold breeze was blowing and I had no jacket. My head was down as I walked quickly to get inside the terminal. My wife had decided that she would be the one to pick me up. I traipsed right past her without recognizing her. She was nine months pregnant when we last saw each other. She had short hair throughout the entire time that I had known her, but at that time her hair was long and frosted. She had to call me back after I had strolled past. I have no memory of any hugs or conversation on the drive back home. We had rented the second floor of my parent's house for the previous three and a half years. When we walked into my mother's living room on the first floor, my sister, Mary, was there with baby Lee. My wife picked him up and placed him into my arms. That was the first glimpse of my son who was then over two months old. As I cradled him in my arms, he looked up at me, threw up, and began to cry. Everyone laughed as I handed him back and headed up-stairs to bed. I slept for nearly sixteen hours then awoke to the worst hangover that I have ever had. Since that hopelessly wasted experience, I have neither been inebriated nor con-sumed any hard liquor. I spent the next five days visiting Lee at my sister's home. Besides Lee, Mary also had a nine-month-old baby boy of her own to care for. I set up an allotment for her from my military pay to care for Lee until my Vietnam tour would be over. Though I stayed with my wife, we had limited time together. She had to work at her secretarial job during the entire time of my leave. Suffice it to say, we were not able to address any of our problems. Before I knew it, I was flying from Pittsburgh back to McChord Air Force Base for the seemingly endless transport back to Cam Ranh Bay. I succeeded in ac-quiring a place on the flight manifest of a troop transport leav-ing one minute past midnight the day after I had arrived at McChord Air Force Base. Those planes always took off a min-ute or so past midnight to prevent one additional day of com-bat pay entitlement for the deploying troops. My assigned plane was a chartered Douglas Super DC-8 capable of carrying approximately 250 passengers. We were ordered to assemble in the small waiting terminal an hour or more prior to our board-ing time. Seating was according to rank. Typically, two to five officers were assigned to the front-most seats. As a captain, I had an aisle seat in the first row. There were two to three seats on either side of a very long center aisle. Lavatories were avail-able in the rearmost portion of the cabin. We left the ground a minute or two past midnight and flew for four hours to our first refueling stop. As we approached Anchorage, Alaska, a severe storm prevented us from landing. Consequently, our crew was forced to turn around and fly back to Seattle. After flying for eight hours, we landed at the Seattle-Tacoma International Airport instead of McChord Air Force Base. Once our plane had landed, we deplaned and were bussed to a Holiday Inn at the airport for billeting. That beautiful hotel had just been built but had not yet officially opened. We were assigned two men to a room. We were authorized two beers and two meals per day and were ordered not to leave the building. That truly was a government miscalculation to house 250 GIs on their way to war in a brand-new hotel. I was billeted in a first-floor room along with another captain assigned to the US Army. At one point, he and I were conversing while viewing the airport runways from the large picture window in our room when suddenly a TV set dropped from the floor above, shot past our window, and shattered on the sidewalk outside. Suffice it to say, those rowdy young soldiers trashed that facility in less than two days. Later that evening, we were loaded onto busses and transported back to the aerial port at McChord AFB to await another Super DC-8 to convey us to Vietnam. Since there was already an additional troop transport plane scheduled to head to Vietnam that night, the small aerial port waiting area was packed beyond its capacity. Such transport planes were scheduled almost every night. Nearly five hundred of us mulled around for a couple of hours looking for a place to sit down. Though alcohol was forbidden, there were quite a few hipflasks and pint bottles being passed around. I clearly remember one individual who stood out in the crowd. He was an Army sergeant major and the most decorated individual whom I have ever seen. Besides campaign ribbons from World War II, Korea, and Vietnam, he displayed a Combat Infantry Badge with two stars. His top awards certainly signaled him out as a war hero. Unfortunately, he was being redeployed yet again to fight in an unpopular war where the American public had turned against our soldiers instead of the politicians responsible for that war. After draining the last of his flask, he disappeared into the men's room. Eventually his troops missed him and discovered that he had passed out on the pot in a locked stall. Because of his height, they were unable to pull him out beneath the enclosure wall. Finally, a short, wiry soldier from his unit managed to squeeze under the wall and unlock the door. As his troops uprighted him, his large ribbon display had partially disconnected but remained on his uniform at an angle. His valorous unit award chords worn over his shoulder had also become detached and hung down to his knee on that side. As to be expected, two Air Force security policemen escorted him out of the terminal...not under arrest but, out of respect for the gallant individual that he was, he was taken to a room somewhere to sober up and await the next day's flight. As midnight approached, we passengers from the flight that had returned from Alaska two days earlier boarded the first of the two waiting troop carriers.

TYPICAL CABIN VIEW OF A SUPER DC-8 TROOP TRANSPORT.

Once we were aboard, the remaining passengers in the terminal, who were the ones originally scheduled to leave that night
were directed to occupy the second plane. Both planes had un-
remarkable journeys to Anchorage for refueling. We were on
the ground for an hour. Everything in that terminal was closed.
I spent the time gazing at an awesome stuffed record polar
bear on display in the airport concourse. Once both planes had
been refueled and reloaded, they taxied to the main runway. I
was seated in the first row of the first of the two planes. We
left the ground without incident and headed for our next refueling stop in Japan. A few minutes later, as the second plane
attempted to take off, there was a minor explosion in the rear
of the plane. Witnesses reported that it was travelling too
slow to climb and too fast to land. As the plane came down the
extended tail section apparently collided first. It broke free
from the rest of the plane and shattered. That was followed by

additional small explosions and a severe fire. Forty-six passengers and a civilian stewardess all perished in that tail section. Once the plane had come to a stop, survivors from the rest of the plane were reported as having run in all directions to escape the burning fuel and additional small explosions. Though reports varied, it seemed that none of the survivors suffered severe injuries. The first plane, which carried me, continued across the Pacific, and landed at Tachikawa Air Force Base as expected for refueling. After deplaning for the expected hour layover, we were surprised that the second plane did not arrive shortly after us as scheduled. We were delayed in Japan for a considerable amount of time while those in charge tried to sort out what had happened. We eventually got word of a crash but no details. Panic spread through the passengers of my plane. Many were friends with and assigned to the same units as passengers of the ill-fated second plane. We wandered about that aerial port for over four hours fearing the worst for our military brothers. Suddenly we were both surprised and confused by news that another military transport plane had just arrived from Anchorage, Alaska. As the passengers deplaned from that flight, there was lots of hugging and hand shaking. From the numbers, it was clear that most of the survivors, after a cursory medical check were quickly boarded onto another chartered Super DC-8 and shuffled back off to the war in Vietnam. One can only speculate on the PTSD rate among those survivors. They were not even given time to catch their breath after what had just happened to them. Passengers on my flight were only given a brief time for reassurance that most of their brothers at arms had survived. We were then reseated in our plane to continue the last leg of our journey to Cam Ranh Bay.

FIRE CONTROL WAS DIFFICULT BECAUSE OF WHERE THE PLANE HAD COME TO A STOP AND THE FACT THAT THE FUEL TANKS HAD JUST BEEN FILLED.

TRAIL OF THE BURNING FUEL AND TAIL SECTION PHOTOGRAPHED FROM THE AIR DAYS LATER FOLLOWING CRASH DEBRIS REMOVAL.

Big Cat and Bob Moles picked me up at Cam Ranh Bay's fourteenth USAF Aerial Port and chauffeured me back to the
Beachcomber (our hooch). I never heard any more about the
crash survivors. They were probably loaded onto buses and
carted off to the Army barracks at Cam Ranh Bay to await their
assignments. In the end, I had to wait many months to return
home, retrieve baby Lee from my sister and learn how to be
a single dad. A great deal had happened during my two-week
break from the war that has had a lasting impact on my life.

EPILOGUE

The conclusion of this memoir occurred some fifteen years after the tragic plane crash recounted above. At that time, I was stationed at Travis Air Force Base in Northern California and had been appointed as a member of an Air Force forensic identification team. This was still a time when DNA identification was not available for mass casualty scenarios. That left forensic dentistry as the primary identification instrument for such large-scale disasters. My appointment required attendance at a week-long forensic dentistry course presented by the Armed Forces Institute of Pathology (AFIP). There were exercises during the course where attendees had to confirm identifications based on examinations of bone and dental remains of actual victims from three catastrophic plane crashes:

1. The first group of specimens were collected from the most devastating air disaster of all time...the March 27, 1977, crash at Tenerife in the Canary Islands. A dense, murky fog

had shrouded the runway offering less than 1,000 feet of visibility. Pan Am Airlines Flight 1736 and Royal Dutch Airlines Flight 4805 had both been refueled and were taxiing for take-off when they collided on the runway. Both planes were Boeing 747 passenger airliners. 583 passengers and crew members were killed. Only sixty-one victims of the crash had survived.

2. The second group of specimens were gathered from the demolished remains of a crash site in Poland. On March 14, 1980, a chartered flight from New York to Warsaw had impacted on final approach. The plane carried the entire US Boxing Team and support staff which had been scheduled to compete there in two international events. All seventy-seven passengers and crew aboard the plane perished.

3. The final group of specimens were gleaned from the loss of a US Military chartered Douglas Super DC-8 which occurred in late 1970. The plane's capacity was 250 passengers. It was transporting 219 Army and Air Force troops as well as ten crew members from McChord Air Force Base, Washington to Cam Ranh Bay Air Force Base, Vietnam. Most

passengers were young draftees. The plane crashed upon takeoff following a refueling stop at Anchorage, Alaska. Forty-six passengers and one stewardess lost their lives. The extended tail section exploded, broke off, and shattered as the plane came down. That was followed by additional small explosions and a severe fuel fire. That was the plane crash that I had just missed back in 1970 as I returned to Vietnam after a humanitarian leave.

As I sat there holding the dentate half mandible that I had just used to identify a young victim, I could not help but ponder the fact that he and I sat together in that crowed aerial port at McChord Air Force Base for two or more hours awaiting our flights. We may have even sat next to each other. Were it not for seat assignments, over which we had no control, I could have been assigned to that second ill-fated plane.

RAINING ROCKETS

The city of Nha Trang was located on the coast of South Vietnam approximately twenty-three and a half miles north of Cam Ranh Bay Air Force Base. An Air Force base had been established there in 1951 as a French pilot and navigator training center for the South Vietnamese Air Force. By 1955, it had become the South Vietnamese Air Force Academy. Beginning in the late 1960s, the US Air Force used it as a special operations base. There was a small USAF dispensary on the base which had been assembled using small, interconnected modular steel buildings. Among the buildings was a two-chair dental clinic. No Air Force dentists were stationed there. The clinic was manned by two Air Force NCOs. Each month, a dentist stationed at Cam Ranh Bay made a temporary duty (TDY) trip to Nha Trang to spend two days handling dental emergencies and updating dental examinations. Personnel needing definitive or advanced dental care were temporarily sent to the Air Force dental clinic at Cam Ranh Bay. For some unknown reason, the water supply at the Nha Trang Clinic was turned off each day around noon which allowed time for the visiting dentist to explore the nearby city of Nha Trang (a former French resort city). Usually, those appealing monthly trips to Nha Trang were shared by the senior dental officers stationed at the Cam Ranh Bay Dental Clinic. As a reward for the few young captains who volunteered for MEDCAP missions, our names were added to the Nha Trang rotation roster. I was very grateful and excited when my name finally made it to the top of the rotation list. Little did I know that that trip would provide my most terrifying night in Vietnam.

My trip to Nha Trang was via my first flight aboard a C-123 transport plane. I was a very inexperienced flier. My first flight ever occurred at age twenty-six (less than six months earlier) when I flew to Sheppard AFB for my basic training. The flight from Cam Ranh Bay to Nha Trang was usually completed within about twenty minutes. But that day, we were airborne for over an hour. We kept circling through clouds. There was no visibility out of the plane's windows. I must admit, I was getting a bit nervous. I was aware that the C-123 planes had a reputation for untoward mishaps. They were significantly underpowered compared to their incredible successor, the C-130 transport. When we finally touched down, we were told that all air traffic had been halted to accommodate the arrival of a visiting US senator. All was well. I was ushered to the dental clinic where I saw patients until the water was shut off just past twelve o'clock. The two NCOs there were great and invited me to ride with them to see the sites in central Nha Trang. On the way, we drove past the spectacular statue of Buddha seated on a low hill. I had planned to go back there the next day for better pictures and possible entry into that magnificent monument, but that was never meant to be. We spent the afternoon walking the city's streets and market places. That day was my only opportunity to experience life in a Vietnamese city.

ON THE TOP IS MY ORIGINAL PICTURE OF THE MAGNIFICENT
NHA TRANG SHRINE OF BUDDHA IN 1970. BELOW IS
A CURRENT PICTURE OF THE SAME IDOL.

TYPICAL BUSTLING NHA TRANG STREET SCENES IN 1970.
THE GIRLS IN WHITE *AO-DAI* DRESS ARE STUDENTS.

Early next morning I was back on the job in the cramped dental clinic looking forward to another trip downtown. By midday the water supply had been shut off as expected. Following a quick clinic clean-up, we climbed into a Jeep and headed downtown. On the way we passed a rather large communication center on our right that sat about fifty yards or so back from the road. It covered three to four acres and was surrounded by very tall, double chain link fences topped with plenty of concertina wire for security. The site contained several of what appeared to be large radar screens and lots of tall antenna towers. Just as we were approaching that area, several rockets hit within and around that enclosure. The NCO driving our Jeep immediately made a U-turn and sped back to our base. Standing orders were for all personnel to stand by in situations like this in case they were needed to help with casualties. But none came to our dispensary. As the day drew to a close, I found myself sitting with three NCOs on the back steps of the main dispensary module...sipping a can of Budweiser. A Dodge crackerbox ambulance was parked next to us on the small, otherwise empty asphalt parking lot behind the clinic. A massive pile of sand sat at far the edge of the parking lot to our right. A couple of coiled concertina wire fences separated the parking lot from a row of earth covered bunkers approximately twenty-five yards in front of us. The bunkers were part of the adjacent US Army Green Beret Camp which had been turned over to the South Vietnamese Rangers that very day. Between that camp and the Central Highlands rising in the distance was an enormous, crowded civilian settlement of shacks and houses. Every so often, a single rocket would crash into that area of shanties raising lots of smoke, debris, and dust. At the same time, Huey gunships were spraying the distant hillsides. Their rate of fire was impressively fast. Those mini-guns sounded like a loud air horn rather than a machine gun. Though only every fifth shot was a tracer bullet, they formed a solid red line in the sky like a laser beam due to their extreme velocity. When the tracers hit the ground, the ricochets resembled a Fourth of July sparkler. Apparently, the enemy's display of force was in response to the Green Beret camp's transfer to the Vietnamese army. As dusk approached, the frequency of the rocket strikes increased. At one point, one of the NCOs seated two steps above me leaned over and suggested that that the enemy was walking the rockets closer to where we were sitting in an effort to hit the ammunition bunkers in front of us.

Someone had once told me that a close incoming rocket sounded like a freight train. No sooner had that NCO voiced his opinion about the rockets getting closer than we all heard that freight train. From my seat on the bottom step, I instinctively rolled under the parked ambulance as I heard a deafening blast. A blinding cloud of dust surrounded us. Miraculously, the rocket had buried itself in the huge sand pile to our right. The three NCOs had been sitting above me on the steps. All were a bit older than me and a bit overweight. As I looked up from under the ambulance, I saw all three chubby guys struggling and elbowing each other to get through the single dispensary door. It looked like a scene from a Three Stooges movie. We were all fine but agreed that the better part of valor was to stop sipping beer while watching the war and to seek shelter inside. We spent that night in a large open dormitory room containing single beds arranged in rows (similar to a hospital ward). We all slept wearing our flak jackets and helmets. I never actually slept. Throughout the night, we heard the booms of incoming rocket strikes about every ten minutes...some distant, some close...but none hit our dispensary or those bunkers just behind us. We certainly received our share of enemy rockets at Cam Ranh Bay but they always came at night. There were never more than two or three before the Korean White Horse Division (assigned as the front line of defense of the peninsula) peppered the highlands launch site of the rockets with howitzer rounds. That sleepless night in Nha Trang fortunately was the only time that I had experienced such intense, round the clock bombardment.

MY FIRST HUEY RIDE (BELL UH-1 IROQUOIS)
FROM NHA TRANG TO CAM RANH BAY.

Very early the next morning, I was driven to the flight line and a waiting medevac helicopter. That was my first ever ride in a Huey. They seated me at the end of the back bench seat on the port side. As I was getting seated quite a few passengers began to arrive. Some were patients heading for the Cam Ranh Bay AF Hospital. A few others were guys heading home or on to their two-week R&R (rest and relaxation). The chopper was so packed with passengers that I wondered if it would be able take off. Once airborne, we flew very low and straight out to sea where we would be out of small arms range. I was impressed with how low we were flying. The seas were very rough that day with lots of exceptionally high waves. Shortly after takeoff, the crowd in the center of the cabin would give out an occasional cheer. I soon realized that the cheers were for the pilot kissing the white caps with the chopper's skids. The pilot and copilot were very young and fearless Army warrant officers. As satisfying as it was to have had my first chopper ride. I was elated to have my boots back on the sands of the dune.

I had requested duty in Vietnam as my first active-duty appointment. It was not because of my belief in the war but my intention of doing something positive to support our soldiers sent there to fight that unpopular war. The American press had turned the country against our troops instead of the politicians and wartime industrialists responsible for the war. So many of my childhood friends had been drafted and sent there to fight. In 1969, a cousin had been killed in combat. In addition, I had wanted to do something positive for Vietnamese people suffering the ravages of that war in their countryside villages. News of the 1968 My Lai massacre had an immense impact on me. My intentions for volunteering were realized at our clinic with what seemed to be an endless supply of dental emergencies, extractions, and carious teeth needing treatment. In addition, I had ample opportunities to volunteer for MEDCAP missions in the bush to help Vietnamese civilians. All seemed to be working out as I had hoped. But I had not yet learned an important element of military wisdom...NEVER, NEVER, NEVER VOLUNTEER! While lying on my cot that night in Nha Trang wearing a helmet and flack vest as it was raining rockets, I could not help but ask myself..."What the fuck was I thinkin'?"

SUNDAY MILK RUNS

Early Monday morning, following my arrival in Vietnam, I began my in-processing. This was accomplished at multiple
stations (in separate buildings) where all records were developed on paper by hand. There were stations for personnel, fi-
nance, medical, billeting and even supply for issue of our jungle
fatigues and boots. The waiting lines were insufferable. Then
we had to wait in additional lines to open a bank account and
get a post office box. All of this, of course, was done under a
sweltering tropical sun accompanied by what must have been
100 percent humidity. This all occurred over our first few days
in country. While lost somewhere in the line at the personnel
office, I struck up a conversation with an Air Force first lieutenant just ahead of me in that impatient column of GIs. He
was a recent US Air Force Academy graduate and copilot on a
C-7 Caribou crew. However, his ultimate educational ambition
was to become a dentist. That gave us plenty to talk about. We
seemed to make a very quick connection and during the following weeks, he invited me, as my schedule would allow, to

join him and his crew on their supply runs to the various fire bases throughout the highlands in central and northern South Vietnam. What an opportunity that was to see the country beyond the confines of Cam Ranh Bay peninsula. Every five to six weeks, we junior general dentists were assigned DOD (24 hour on call) duty for a week. Except for those weeks, my Sundays were usually free to relax, drink alcoholic refreshments or fly on a Caribou if they had a run scheduled. On average, I was able to make a milk run with my flight line friends once every four to six weeks.

The C-7 Caribou was a small, twin engine turboprop transport plane. They were a remarkable workhorse that served US jungle and Central Highland firebases exceptionally well. They could carry up to thirty-two passengers, up to twenty litter patients, or 8,740 pounds of cargo. Though their maximum speed was 216 mph, their cruising speed was around 120 mph. The greatest ability of these star performing aircraft was their ability to take off and land on very short, poorly developed jungle runways. Though statistics vary, available information reports that they could take off on a 450-foot runway and land on less than six hundred feet. I discovered that many runways at mountain top fire bases did not appear as runways at all. Typically, these milk runs carried both GIs as well as foreign national passengers. Cargo consisted of food, howitzer and small arms ammunition, and mail. Only 307 of these remarkable bush transports were built between 1958 and 1968. Because of the insufferable Vietnamese heat and humidity, missions were often flown with the rear cargo door open. That along with the

assistance of a gunner's safety belt afforded me a great opportunity for photographs.

MY FIRST CARIBOU FLIGHT WAITING FOR BOARDING.

TAXIING FOR TAKEOFF.

VIEW FROM REAR LOADING DOOR OF A C-7 CARIBOU UPON TAKEOFF.

MY VIEW OF THE COCKPIT WHILE STANDING ON THE CREW CHIEF'S
STEP. SOMETIMES ON CARGO FLIGHTS WITHOUT ANY PASSENGERS, THE
CREW CHIEF WOULD LET ME WEAR HIS HEADPHONES AND STAND ON THE
STEPS BETWEEN THE PILOT AND COPILOT SEATS FOR GREAT VISIBILITY
WHILE HE SAT ON A BENCH SEAT JUST INSIDE THE PLANE'S CABIN.

JUST AFTER TAKEOFF OVER CHECK POINT CHARLIE,
THE BRIDGE THAT JOINED CAM RANH BAY PENINSULA
WITH THE SOUTH VIETNAMESE MAINLAND.

BA NGOI ON THE MAINLAND WHERE WE PERFORMED
MOST OF OUR MEDCAP MISSIONS.

HEADING INTO "CHARLIE'S COUNTRY",
THE VIETNAMESE CENTRAL HIGHLANDS.

As I was perched on the crew chief's step between the pilot and copilot during my first milk run flight, the pilot asked me if I would like to see a combat landing. I did not think that he was referring to the tiny encampment just ahead. There did not appear to be a landing strip. At the time, we were cruising at about ten thousand feet over the fire base pictured to the right. As soon as I nodded yes, he put the plane into a dive that seemed to be heading straight into the ground. Just before I was sure that we would crash, somehow, he miraculously leveled the plane out and I could feel us touch down pretty hard. He immediately reversed the propellers to aid in braking which raised a blinding cloud of red dust. Visibility out any windows including the pilot's windshield was zero. Somehow the plane came to a stop. That had to be my greatest adrenaline rush of all time. Since the rear loading door was already open, troops on the ground entered up the open ramp and quickly unloaded our cargo. I sat down and stayed out of their way. As soon as they had finished, our pilot turned the craft around and prepared for takeoff. The engines were never shut down for this short stop. After an exceptionally short approach down a bumpy red dirt runway, we were again airborne and heading for the next firebase.

HOW DOES ONE LAND A CARIBOU TRANSPORT
ON THIS MOUNTAINTOP FIRE BASE?

That one was larger and armed with 105 mm howitzers. It was surrounded by a more even terrain which had been stripped of nearly all vegetation (probably with the assistance of Agent Orange which contaminated any surface water used for drinking and washing). In addition to the danger of defending such an installation, grunts usually survived on C rations and slept on the ground or in sand bagged trenches.

ANOTHER FIREBASE WHERE TERRAIN WAS STRIPPED
OF VEGETATION BY AGENT ORANGE.

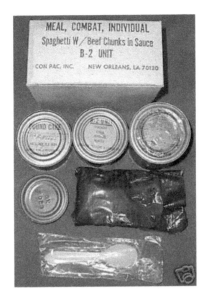

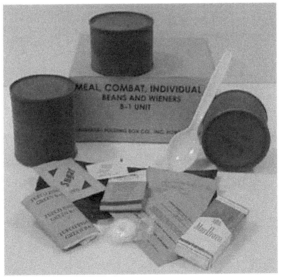

TYPICAL VIETNAM WAR ERA C RATIONS. SOME INCLUDED SMALL
CIGARETTE PACKS, MATCHES, AND CHEWING GUM. SOME WERE
AWFUL BUT I DID LOVE THE POUND CAKE. GRUNTS IN THE FIELD
USUALLY SURVIVED ON THESE AND A RATION OF BEER.

TYPICAL SCENES OF HAMLETS AND WATERWAYS
ON THE SUNDAY CARIBOU MILK RUNS.

The purpose of this memoir is not to present an anthology of the sights and adventures that I was allowed to experience on my free Sundays. These flights got me out of the large base camps on the peninsula and into the countryside to see first-hand how our warriors (many of whom were my patients) had to survive from day to day. This is a humble attempt to pay tribute to the dedicated air crews who bravely flew low and slow in unarmed transports to support our warriors stationed at remote and dangerous fire bases. They carried all sorts of cargo, from rations and mail to explosive artillery rounds. They flew in all kinds of weather, including the incessant deluge of the rainy season. Despite the inherent dangers involved in many of their missions, they often were never recognized for their crucial endeavors. This is also an attempt to highlight the grunts stationed in those remote bush outposts. They faced the dangers of direct enemy assault, shelling, and booby traps daily. They had to suffer through sweltering heat and humidity while surviving on C rations and a daily ration of beer. Depending on the time of year, they had to slog through endless tropical monsoon rains and nearly impenetrable mud. By the late 1960s, their service and sacrifice in Southeast Asia was being ignored and even condemned by many of their fellow countrymen as well as the American press.

LOW ALTITUDE VIEWS OF THE CENTRAL HIGHLANDS WERE BREATHTAKING. THIS WAS A SCENE HEADING SOUTH TOWARD SAIGON EARLY ONE SUNDAY MORNING.

Many Vietnam veterans upon returning home were shamed at airports and often met with jeers. They were called baby killers. Some were egged and spat upon. People in general never said "welcome home." No one ever asked about Vietnam and no one ever seemed to care. Perhaps the greatest insult came from president Carter when he granted amnesty to all the draft dodgers who fled the country during the time of the Vietnam conflict.

The first time that someone actually said the words "welcome home" to me was thirty-two years after I had returned home. Those words were spoken by three other Vietnam veterans who were members of a motorcycle club that I was inquiring about. Their "welcome home" brought tears to my eyes. After fifty plus years, there are still many homeless Vietnam vets, as well as those suffering from PTSD and the ravages of Agent Orange. In closing this memoir, I implore readers to say a simple "welcome home" when you see an old vet wearing a Vietnam Veteran hat or t-shirt. It will mean more than you could ever imagine.

RANDOM MEMORIES OF VIETNAM '70–'71

I remember:

- the incessant chopping of Hueys overhead.

- a hooch called Beachcomber.

- going to the Post Office two or three times a day.

- the unsettling thud of incoming and immediate answering reports of the Koreans' 105s.

- visits to the Korean White Horse Division fire base at Cam Ranh Bay and drinking O B beer with those incredible soldiers.

- the stench of *Nuoc Mam* in the Comber after Do Ti ate her rice.

- the eerie sight of countless roach antennae waving between the shit house wall boards.

- the sheer luxury of a hot shower.

- the insufferable humidity.

- "numbah one, numbah ten, and numbah ten thousand."

- standing in lines...everywhere!

- living on letters from home.

- the sulfurous odor of our water.

- the acrid smell of burning shit and JP4.

- black beetle nut teeth waving in the breeze......on MEDCAP.

- Miss Hai (the hospital librarian) in her white *ao-dai* walking by and taking my breath away.

- that uncomfortable feeling pissing into the clinic urinal while carrying on a conversation with Dien, the clinic *mama-san*, washing our smocks next to me in the men's room sink.

- sand......everywhere.

- the "Merry Molesmobile," the Jeep we "commandeered" from the flight line and all the places where it carried us.

- the abandoned WW II Japanese bunkers that lined the shores of Cam Ranh Peninsula.

- "ain't no biggies on the dune."

- ration cards.

- Dong, Pee, and MPCs.

- that filthy bowl of malaria pills at the end of every chow line.

- that great pizza at the South Beach Army O' Club.

- being "Tee-Tee Dinky Dau."

- watching our plaques move up the waiting room wall as we got closer to our DEROS.

- incredible sunsets.

- arriving at a true understanding of the term rainy season.

- the maggots and stench of my first body IDs.

- lighting charcoal with JP4.

- driving that damned old Dodge crackerbox to Ba Gnoi on MEDCAP Tuesdays.

- that nasty pan of zephiran chloride at the end of a MEDCAP mission.

- my first Huey ride, a dust off so crowded that I feared we would never leave the ground.

- trying to grow my first moustache.

- becoming a father for the first time just weeks after arriving in country but not seeing my precious son for months.

- my Christmas Dear John telegram......that fu#%*in' bitch.

- watching C-119s spray Agent Orange around the base and how quickly the foliage crumbled.

- persistent pouring through the PACEX catalog.

- never getting used to warm beer.

- rocket damage.

- short-timer calendars.

- firing my two rounds from a 105.

- the delectable hamburgers at NAF.

- the typhoon of '71 and looking up through its eye.

- body bags on the flight line.

- the agonizing headaches that I got from San Miguel Beer.

- the gazillion pounds of amalgam that I plugged.

- Stanley the turtle.

- "No sweat *Bac Si.*"

- twenty-five cent haircuts.

- "Boo Koo Boom Boom."

- hopping Caribou milk runs on Sundays.

- taking aerial photos from an open Caribou loading door.

- watching "Combat" reruns on AFVN-TV.

- filling sand bags.

- CCR playing in the background all day long in the clinic.

- eating dog at Bekins Air Van parties.

- "Puff the Magic Dragon" and tracers on the hillsides.

- bartering......for everything imaginable.

- C ration pound cake.......my favorite.

- Judy Collins breathing life into my Teac tape deck and Sansui speakers with her "Damned Old Rodeo".

- proudly hanging Vietnam film canisters from my camera strap.

- mismatched tread patterns on my jungle boots.

- Check-point Charlie and the bridge to the mainland.

- The Red Light Inn...... enough said......

- the overwhelming sensation of power the first time that I fired a .50 caliber.

- the awe of a napalm strike.

- Sunday afternoon cock fights on RMK Hill where we later barbecued and ate the losing birds.

- cheap booze and too much of it.

- SOS for breakfast every Tuesday morning and......if we were lucky, leftover SOS on Wednesday mornings.

- ox carts and three wheeled taxis on Highway 1.

- *Baby-sans* in straw hats and white *ao-dais*.

- running from the Comber to the latrine the two times I had dysentery......I didn't make it a few times.

- abandoned Amerasian orphans.

- hooch maids washing our dishes, fatigues, and themselves in that same big tub of water (and in that order).

- the hospital outdoor theater with a plywood screen and bleachers.

- the magnificent Buddha at Nha Trang.

- the sounds, filth, and stench of the Ba Gnoi marketplace.

- *Di di mau* from MEDCAP when Charlie was coming.

- Dust offs off-loading wounded and body bags.

- Vietnamese houses sheathed in flattened beer cans.

- being young once......and fit.

- the usefulness of a P-38 can opener.

- Big Cat's mint AK-47 that we kept in the Comber.

- the "pucker factor" of a rocket attack.

- stealing those bananas from the trees around the BX...... Hey! We did put them to good use in that blender.

- reading Stars & Stripes.

- the old French monastery at Myca Village.

- live shows at the O Club...My favorite was that little Pilipino guy who sounded just like Johnny Cash.

- smoke filled Tiger Air Line Super DC-8s.

- miles and miles of concertina wire.

- the language of war......the acronyms and slang like: BOHICA, FUBAR, FIGMO, DILLIGAF, Zoomies, MAC-Tunas, Lifers, LBFM, and on and on...

- pissing out our hooch front door during the rainy season.

- my hooch mates to whom I'll always be bound, *di wees* all.

- the enormous red and blue lizards on K-9 Hill and how they would dash out of the brush for a handful of dog food.

- planning my stereo and camera systems...for months.

- buying all that useless monkey pod stuff.

- thanking God for that dedicated cadre of military nurses and Doughnut Dollies.

- the dog handlers of K-9 Hill.

- placing gold crowns on a sentry dog's teeth and getting my ass chewed for it.

- getting shelled all night long on my first TDY at Nha Trang.

- black bras and French bread.

- that stinky old turtle shell that hung on the Comber wall.

- precious pictures from home.

- badly outdated clinic supplies like local anesthesia from the Korean War.

- how that shanty town near Cam Ranh City seemed to grow weekly like mold on bad bread.

- R&R stories.

- how the smell of Vietnam followed us home in our hold baggage.

- *Xin loi.*

- how the undercurrent at the Officer's beach managed to kill......was it six people? ......in November of 1970, before they closed it for a while.

- how we always had an audience on MEDCAP and how they'd cheer if one of our patients moaned or cried out in pain.

- how the true currency in Vietnam was a case of steaks.

- taking lots and lots of pictures......which I now treasure and occasionally peruse.

- the Freedom Birds and lots of cheering.

- a lonely and hostile homecoming.

- waiting around thirty-five years for someone to say "welcome home" or "thank you for your service."

- visiting the Wall for the first time...and losing it.

- but mostly I remember the fellowship and comfort of the Comber.

Milton Keynes UK
Ingram Content Group UK Ltd.
UKHW020753191023
430857UK00002B/17